Finding Mrs. Hyde
Writing Your First Popular Novel

Margarite St. John

Finding Mrs. Hyde
Writing Your First Popular Novel

Copyright 2011
All rights reserved.

No part of this book may be reproduced or stored in a retrieval system, or transmitted in any form or by any means, electronic, mechanical, photocopying, recording, or otherwise, without express written permission of the author.

www.margaritestjohn.com

This book was previously published as an e-Book through Kindle in a shorter format with a different title: *Finding Mrs. Hyde: How to Write the Mystery Novel You've Been Meaning to Write: A Tip Sheet for First-Time Women Authors*

Cover design by Sara Norwood, www.norwoodarts.com.

Other Books by Margarite St. John

FICTION:
Face Off
Monuments to Murder
Murder for Old Times' Sake

NON-FICTION:
Finding Mrs. Hyde:
How to Write the Mystery Novel You've Been Meaning to Write
A Tip Sheet for First-Time Women Authors
(original title on Kindle)

Our Loyal Readers Say About:

Face Off

"I really enjoyed *Face Off*. It is far better than James Patterson, Patricia Cornwell & Stuart Woods I also read over the past few months. I have recommended it to friends!"
- Jamie

"*Face Off* is easy and enjoyable reading. . . . The pace compelled me to read just one more chapter. . . . A good mystery with an explosive beginning and end."
- A fan, Marco Island

"*Face Off* is well-written and fast-paced. It's kind of a twisted romance as well as a murder mystery. The characters are thoroughly fleshed out, which is different from a lot of mystery novels. . . . I like the way the books ends. Surprising and very exciting."
- Anne-Marie

"The author has given us interesting characters involved in a compelling story line. An easy comfortable writing style keeps you involved and draws you on, chapter to chapter. I'm left wishing for more!"
- pageturner

"Couldn't put the book down! Extremely well-written with a suspenseful plot and interesting characters. Each chapter ended with a hook, so I couldn't wait to start the next one! All of the requirements of a great suspense novel were woven into the book with great thought. A definite must-read! I can't wait to read more from this author!"
- Heather

Monuments to Murder

"It took me only two days to read this book. It was funny, disturbing, educational, enlightening, and ended with a good twist. I'm hooked on this author."
- Anne-Marie

"This is the second book from this author that I have read and I absolutely loved it!! Suspenseful, interesting characters with whom it was easy to identify, and a plot that was both intriguing and yet easy to follow. I literally could not put down my Kindle for 2 days until I finished it! I would say that this author has exactly what it takes to please the suspense novel fan and keep them coming back for more! Can't wait to read her next novel."
- Heather

Murder for Old Times' Sake

"The characters are very interesting, the story compelling, and the who-done-it suspense kept me reading to the funny and fitting end. The author fleshes out the good guys, bad guys, and the somewhere in-betweens, as people the reader can sympathize with and understand their motivations and mindsets. I am looking forward to the fourth book."
- Anne-Marie

"Third book from this author that I have read and just a wonderful suspense novel all the way around! Very interesting characters combine with an exiting plot to keep the reader coming back for more. Details are woven in carefully giving the reader the sense that they "are there" as things are happening. Just loved it!"
- Heather

Table of Contents

Part One: Think Commercial

Prologue: We're just like you, only more so.

Tip 1: Find your inner Mrs. Hyde: get comfortable with evil.
Tip 2: Start writing; you're never too old (or too young).
Tip 3: Get over yourself: collaborate if that helps.
Tip 4: Embrace e-readers and on-demand paperbacks; just publish.
Tip 5: Write to sell: choose a popular genre and select a niche.

Part Two: Hook 'Em

Tip 6: Tell a good story, but don't make it the story of your life.
Tip 7: Create compelling characters; don't write about yourself.
Tip 8: Select a classic plot; there aren't a lot to choose from.
Tip 9: Stick with the classic plot structure: beginning, middle, and end.
Tip 10: Hook the reader anyway you can, and there are lots of ways.
Tip 11: Choose a setting you know, but throw in some spice.
Tip 12: Find your voice; speak naturally.
Tip 13: Tell the story chronologically, but tell it from many perspectives.
Tip 14: Focus on dialogue and action, but use narrative when it works.
Tip 15: Don't skip the humor; life is funny.
Tip 16: Catch a rising star with a captivating title.
Tip 17: Keep the prose real and edit viciously: purple is not the new black.

Part Three: Work It

Tip 18: Eating a whole carcass kills the appetite, so just start somewhere.
Tip 19: Forget literary gurus; remember readers like you.
Tip 20: Keep your eyes on the prize, and the main prize isn't money -- really.
Tip 21: Shoot the incubus! Free yourself from doubt.

Glossary of Literary Terms

Part One: Think Commercial

A best-seller was a book which somehow sold well because it was selling well.

Daniel J. Boorstin

Prologue: We're just like you

*Only more so.

We are two sisters in Fort Wayne, Indiana, who have co-authored and published three mystery novels and are now writing a fourth. We complete a work of fiction in six months. We divide up the duties. The younger sister is the Storyteller, the older sister the Scribe (see **Tip 3**). Our functions overlap, and both of us edit.

Most of our readers are women who read lots of mystery novels. Some of them have remarked that they too have always thought of writing a novel but don't know how to get started or are afraid to. We didn't know much four years ago either, but we've learned a lot in the process. This deliberately short tip sheet is intended to help them -- and you -- write a popular, or genre, novel for a commercial market and then get it published as an e-book or on-demand paperback.

The kind of fiction we're talking about goes by a number of names: commercial, genre, or popular fiction, as opposed to "literary" fiction. For literary fiction, think William Faulkner, Ernest Hemingway, and Norman Mailer. For genre fiction, think of Arthur C. Clarke (science fiction), Zane Grey (western), Stephanie Meyer (vampire/horror), J. K. Rowling (fantasy), Patricia Cornwell (mystery), and Georgette Heyer (historical romance).   Genre fiction includes a wide variety of categories, but the familiar ones are romance, adventure, western, fantasy, horror, science fiction, inspirational, and mystery. Genre fiction is described as formulaic, meaning there's a formula or structure that readers expect and enjoy. In our minds, the great thing about genre fiction is that authors don't have to be crazy or tragic or hideously depressed; a little neurotic will do just fine.

These twenty-one tips do not comprise a set of rules. Every rule for writing has been broken by someone anyway, often by geniuses. But if you're new to writing fiction, or if you have a drawer full of unreadable manuscripts, then having a simple way to start thinking about a commercial project helps. We've kept this tip sheet deliberately short so as not to waste your time. You can buy and read much longer guides, but if a subject can be boiled down to its essence, why not start there? We've also confined ourselves to mysteries because that's what we write, though most of what we say applies to all genres.

We have no specific training for writing commercial fiction. Frankly, we don't know what that would be. But we are educated through college and beyond. We have done a lot of non-fiction writing and a lot of living. We have definite views about life. God, family, and country are good. The *New York Times*, the Manson family, and the United Nations are not so good. Because humans are flawed, the emergence of evil is no more surprising than the embodiment of virtue, but it's often more interesting. There are moral principles to live by and immoral principles to shun. Small towns are as interesting as big cities. Humor and murder go together. Every person in the world shares the dual nature of good and evil. Our views necessarily shape our fiction. Yours will too.

When we decided to write murder mysteries, we weren't aiming to impress the literary world or become richer than the Queen of England, though we scorn neither achievement. If you have it in you to become the next Kurt Vonnegut (weird and respected by the literary lights) or J. K. Rowling (rich and popular), you don't need this guide. But if you're not a writer by trade yet want to write genre fiction for commercial publication, we can help you get started with the book that's in your head.

We make no claims to greatness. What we can truthfully claim is that we actually write and publish the books in our heads without spending the rest of our lives fantasizing about it. We also get good reviews. Our experience might help you do the same.

Tip 1

Find your inner Mrs. Hyde

★Get comfortable with evil.

Remember Robert Louis Stevenson's novella *Strange Case of Dr Jekyll and Mr Hyde* (1886)? You probably read it in middle school. Dr. Henry Jekyll, a respectable Victorian doctor and philanthropist, periodically transforms himself into the ugly and violent Mr. Hyde. Eventually, the transformation occurs out of the doctor's control and his alter ego's acts are so vicious and unstoppable that he commits suicide. The story embodies the duality of our nature in which good and evil live side by side. If we don't acknowledge the evil part of our nature, then we perform evil acts while projecting them onto others. Evil, once indulged, may assert itself more frequently and aggressively, beyond our control.

We don't suggest you become Mrs. Hyde. We only mean that as a mystery writer (really, a writer of anything) you must do what Dr. Jekyll could not: acknowledge the evil as well as the good in people so you can create grippingly vivid characters and a powerful story. If that sounds obvious to you, congratulations. You're way ahead of where we were when we wrote our first murder mystery. It was a challenge to make the murderer both outwardly respectable and secretly evil, and even more of a challenge to show the dual nature of the "good" characters.

Human nature is complex and fascinating because it is a

duality. The eternal struggle between good and evil is especially important in murder mysteries, and we have more to say about creating interesting good-and-evil characters in **Tip 7.**

Tip 2

Start writing

*You're never too old (or too young).

When our first mystery novel was published on Kindle, we were, respectively, 55 and 71 years old. We're not getting any younger, but we're still writing about one book every six months.

Age has its value. You have more **time** now. Writing takes concentration, quiet, and blocks of uninterrupted time, conditions that were probably in short supply when you were raising a family or pursuing an arduous career.

Your ideas about good and evil, justice and mercy, sanity and lunacy, common sense and poor judgment are grounded in something more profound than the arrogance of youth, so you're **wiser** than when you emerged from college with the certainty that you knew all there was to know.

And you have more first-hand **experience** with the world than when you were thirty. You've met lots of people, traveled many places, read tons of books, heard every story there is -- and lived some of them -- so you have a gold mine of experiences and memories to draw upon.

This is not to say that young people don't have good stories in their heads. It's merely to remind ourselves that people of a certain age can and should write, and since we're people of a certain age, our focus is on them.

Time, wisdom, and experience mean you're finally ready to tell an entertaining story that means something. Don't anguish about all the lost time. Whatever you write now is going to be better than you'd have written years ago.

One other word: We know writers and readers of popular fiction include men, but for the sake of elegance, we eschew the form he/she and simply treat them all as feminine because we're women and this is our little guide.

Tip 3

Get over yourself

★Collaborate if that helps.

Writing is a lonely business. Even for loners who embrace solitude, sitting for hours at the computer can be daunting. If you have to think of everything, from the big picture to the tiniest details, you risk that dreaded disease of writer's block. And if you can't get over yourself -- and most of us can't -- you won't see the flaws in your story. So consider collaborating by finding a co-author, editor, or sounding board.

As sisters, we don't find it difficult to collaborate. We have a history together. We like each other and often know what the other is thinking before anything is said. We enjoy the companionship. Collaboration comes naturally to us.

More important, we found it was the only way either of us could actually produce a book. The younger sister -- the Storyteller -- loves to make up stories and characters but isn't fond of writing it all down. She comes to the house of the older sister -- the Scribe -- two or three times a week for coffee and starts imagining the next scenes while the Scribe takes notes. Discussion -- really, brain-storming -- is lively, often funny, and always productive.

The Scribe, who loves to write and has the time to do it, then sits down at the computer every day with her notes and her imagination and writes. She gives the draft to the Storyteller for editing, makes the necessary changes, and the process starts again. The Storyteller sees the big picture and therefore knows the last scene of the book right from the outset, and though the Scribe knows too, she concentrates on one scene at a time in chronological order. Sometimes when the Storyteller goes on and on with the plot, the Scribe closes her ears and refuses to take another note.

The greatest benefit of collaboration is something other than companionship, though that's pretty special. Collaboration produces a quality product. It quashes self-indulgence. When the Storyteller makes up a scene that can't be written or strays from the main story, there's someone to tell her so. When the Scribe goes astray with the details, fails to portray a character the way the Storyteller imagined her, or inserts her personal hobbyhorses, there's someone to put her back on course.

We aren't saying you can't write a good book all by yourself. Many people can and do. But it's unusual. Even when a book lists a single author, the acknowledgement page often reveals a long list of helpers -- agents, editors, mentors, proofreaders, expert consultants. But if you don't need or can't find a co-author, at least enlist the help of a sounding board or editor. There's no shame in doing so. And if you like each other a lot, you'll have the time of your lives.

Tip 4

Embrace e-readers and on-demand paperbacks

*Just publish.

The opportunities for first-time authors are greater than ever with the advent of e-books, which now outsell books in paper, and the appearance of CreateSpace, which allows books to be published on demand as paperbacks without the financial burden of carrying a large inventory. No longer is it necessary to find an agent and publisher. For decades, they were the gatekeepers, the filters, helpful in editing and marketing but exacting a big price by diminishing the writer's independence and grabbing the lion's share of the money. Now you can write your book and upload it to, say, Kindle Direct Publishing or CreateSpace.

Before e-books, the chances of getting published were slim indeed. That's particularly true for authors in the Midwest whose values and settings do not appeal to agents and publishers, most of whom work and live on the Coasts.

But the fear of rejection at the hands of the gatekeepers is no longer an excuse for putting off the day you start your book. That doesn't mean you should not try to find an agent if that's your preference. It just means that all is not lost if you fail to interest an agent -- and most unpublished writers do.

Marketing an e-book or on-demand paperback is beyond the scope of this little guide.

Tip 5

Write to sell

★Choose a popular genre.

If you want people to buy and read your novel, choose a popular genre, meaning a category of fiction people really like to read and will spend real money to buy. Almost any story can be structured as a mystery, the only genre we deal with here.

We chose mysteries because women like to read them and we like to write them. Just visit any bookstore to see how much shelf space is devoted to mystery fiction, including all its subcategories: light-hearted crime capers, mysteries of manners and social commentary, hard-boiled and soft-boiled detectives, fictionalized true-crime, political and historical mysteries, police procedurals, suspense, magic realism, cozy mysteries, thrillers, country-house and stormy castle mysteries.

Mysteries written as commercial fiction have obvious advantages.

Advantage One: Sales. Mysteries sell well. They sell so well that by accident or out of curiosity readers will pick up an unknown author because well-known authors can't write fast enough. Thus, even if you've never published anything before, a popular genre gives you a way to find readers.

Advantage Two: Structure. Another advantage of mystery novels accrues to the writer herself. Genre fiction has a structure that confines your story within certain limits while letting your imagination go as wild as you want with the details. The mystery presents normal life interrupted by an evil act that unravels and leads to the punishment of the evil-doer and significant changes in the lives of everyone else. In other words, you start with a skeleton and then drape any flesh on it you want.

Advantage Three: Real Life with a Fantasy Twist. Not to wax too philosophical, there's a third advantage. Genre fiction depicts real life with a fantasy twist, for life is a mystery and doesn't end well, yet we all hope for secret knowledge and some earthly justice while we're here -- which we get in the typical mystery.

Mystery novels are appealing in part because they're scary without being depressing. The threats are manageable because they can be overcome. The central characters experience danger and setbacks, tragedy and loss, but in the end secrets are revealed, justice prevails, and some characters live happily ever after.

Disadvantage. Commercial genre fiction is thought by some writers to have disadvantages, especially the writer who wants to be taken seriously by academics and high-brow reviewers. Kurt Vonnegut, for example, is said to have denied he wrote science fiction so that he would be taken seriously and make more money.

*Select a niche.

Say you decide to write a mystery. Not all the millions of mystery fans will like your book. As we learned in high school where we wanted to be liked by everybody, the wish for universal popularity is never fulfilled. That's okay. Select a niche, or sub-genre, and write for a subset of mystery fans. Readers who like your books will read anything you write, and there will be enough of them to maintain you in ink cartridges and reams of paper and maybe even produce a profit. So, imagine the reader you want to attract.

Are you writing for men or women? Lawyers, stay-at-home moms, or waitresses? Foodies who want recipes with their murder, or fashionistas who relish seeing their heroine in Christian Dior? Techies who want to know how the bomb or chloroform was made? Voyeurs who want to read every detail of a grizzly murder? Church-goers who hate crude language? Homemakers who look forward to cozy scenes in the kitchen? Armchair travelers who crave foreign settings? Social climbers? Art collectors?

Aiming your book at a subset of mystery readers doesn't mean you can't appeal broadly, but it helps in several ways. It keeps you on course, especially with subplots. It constrains your prose in a good way. It helps you flesh out your characters so they seem like real people. If your readers like your dissertations on knitting or Gothic churches, then they'll buy your next book with the expectation of being agreeably entertained the same way.

The danger in, say, focusing on piano recitals or recipes for fresh bread or rehabbing shacks on the beach is that you might bore or irritate your readers by overdoing it, showing off, or sounding preachy. So keep the little dissertations on this or that subject to the minimum that moves the plot or illuminates a character.

Even if you're not a hands-on expert on some subject important to your story -- say, palm reading -- you can consult Wikipedia and Google to learn what you have to know for that touch of authority and realism. Before the Internet, it was difficult, time-consuming, frustrating, and often expensive to research the details that enliven a story. But now it's fun and easy. For our third novel, the Scribe spent half a day on Wikipedia researching palmistry and the Mayan prediction about December 21, 2012 in order to write one small part of one chapter illustrating a character's misplaced reliance on the occult. Tidbits like that enliven the story -- but don't overdo them.

Part Two: Hook 'Em

A successful man is one who can lay a firm foundation with the bricks others have thrown at him.

David Brinkley

Tip 6

Tell a good story

*But don't make it the story of your life.

You have a story to tell. Maybe you want it to be about yourself because your life is staggeringly interesting, stuffed with remarkable coincidences and heroic actions, peopled with incredible characters, unfolding in settings few people know anything about. You've been meaning to write about it for years. If you could just get it into a novel, you know other people would find your life fascinating too.

But novels are fictional stories, not biographies. So tell a good story by taking yourself out of it. This rule might sound counter-intuitive, for aren't we supposed to write about what we know? Yes -- but we all know more than our immediate experience, and our immediate experience is limiting. By all means, use bits and pieces of your life in your book, but they almost certainly need to be refined and embellished to make them interesting. Writers of "literary" fiction sometimes learn this the hard way.

Let's say your parents were alcoholics, or they lost all their money when you were in high school. Your husband is a brute, or he's so soft-hearted everybody takes advantage of him. Your boss is jealous and does everything in his power to spike your career, or you discover he's a clever embezzler. Or too late, you realize you chose the wrong career altogether. Your neighbors and in-laws are lunatics. You're divorced, without money or love, and have to start over. You did a terrible thing in your youth that keeps sabotaging your life. Your children have taken the wrong path in life. You've fallen in love with someone else but don't want to leave your marriage. You're so successful that everyone you think is your friend is actually jealous and vengeful. You're being stalked. You never realized until recently that your sweet uncle Bill was a murderer. Only you know your brother is a drug-dealer and steals from the family business. You suspect your mother is a poisoner. You attend your high school reunion in the hopes of reigniting the spark you once had with the football quarterback. You met your husband under the unlikeliest of circumstances. Your husband just gambled away every last dime you saved for retirement. The abortion you had as a teenager has been revealed just as you're preparing to run for political office. You weren't looking for love but the handsome stranger you met in a bar captured your imagination and your heart.

These are all the germs of good stories, but they're just germs. Remember, there are good germs and bad germs. If you tell the story just as you have experienced it, the bad germs will multiply until they've killed their host. You're too close to the action to tell it well if the story is only about you. You'll keep trying to make yourself the heroine and look better than you are. The other people will become caricatures and the plot stale. The action will be flat and predictable. The climax will disappoint. We've all read books like that, and they're so boring we can't believe they ever got published.

*Story seed

You know you have a good story when you can summarize the main plot in one sentence. A beautiful career woman chooses the wrong man to marry. A mother will do anything to further her daughter's career. A wealthy woman is in danger from greedy friends and relatives. A respectable man's teenage indiscretion complicates the rest of his life. An attractive child is irredeemably evil (a bad seed). A mother's attempt to protect her son actually endangers him.

That one-sentence summary of your story is the seed for everything else. Our term for this is the **story seed**. Unless you can summarize your story in one sentence, you don't yet have a coherent tale.

The story seed can be taken a step further. You can also summarize each of your sub-plots in one sentence. Take our first story seed above as an example. A beautiful career woman chooses the wrong man to marry. One of the eligible men loses his chance when he sleeps with his ex-fiancée. Another eligible man has his mistress killed so she won't ruin his reputation. A minor character, a small-time con man, plans to kill his boss so he can marry the heroine, and the con-man's girlfriend bets on the wrong horse when she agrees to help kill the heroine.

*Theme

The **theme** of a novel is its unifying subject. For purposes of writing a mystery novel, it's useful to think of the theme as the author's moral viewpoint, for mysteries are in effect morality tales. Examples: Loving money is the root of the villain's evil. The villain is so hard-wired to be evil he can't be reformed by human means. Worshipping the idols of her own ambition and her daughter's status leads an anti-heroine to tragedy. Again, unless you can state the theme of your story in one sentence, you don't yet have a coherent tale.

As with the **story seed**, the theme can be taken a step further so that each sub-plot has a different but related theme. Start with the theme that loving money is the root of the villain's evil. Minor character A wants to marry a rich man. Minor character B wants to steal a boat. Minor character C wants to extort money from a Hollywood look-alike. You get the idea.

Tip 7

Create compelling characters

★Don't write about yourself.

The **story seed** -- the one-sentence summary of your story -- tells you who your lead character is. Make her compelling. The temptation is to write yourself into her character. Resist.

By that, we mean, avoid self-love. Don't make the heroine a perfected replica of yourself. Don't get revenge by writing your ex-husband, your father, or your former boss into the villain. Imagine each character as someone different from yourself and everyone you know. That doesn't mean you don't choose characteristics and events you're familiar with. It just means you scramble them, as if putting everything you know about life and people into a food chopper.

Good characters drive the plot, so create them first. The lead or central character is sometimes called the protagonist, either a heroine (or hero) or anti-heroine (or anti-hero), depending on whether she's good or bad. The secondary characters are related to her in some way.

One advantage of using your imagination about the characters is mundane: it avoids lawsuits by people who recognize themselves and aren't happy about it. Friends and family -- even enemies -- are not fair game.

The other advantage is that the characters become interesting once you really let your imagination go wild. Then you can create lives more interesting than your own.

If, for example, your heroine is a career woman, and that's what you are, give her a different career, a different love life, a different family background -- and by all means, give her different sins and virtues from yours and different obstacles to overcome. You won't fall into the trap of writing about yourself.

It's useful to make a list of characters before you start writing. For example: the heroine, her best friend, an old love interest, a new one, a jealous enemy, and the villain. Give them names and write a little of their back story so you can picture them in your head. Don't worry about all the minor characters who may have to make an appearance to keep the plot moving. They'll enter stage right as they're needed.

The creation of the two or three central characters -- the heroine and the villain and perhaps the heroine's love interest -- is where you really let Mrs. Hyde out. The heroine and her love interest have to be likable, more good than bad, but flawed nevertheless. Even the villain may be superficially likable, but he has to be deeply, profoundly flawed.

Heroine first. It's useful to identify with the heroine, at least in some respect, but avoid drawing a self-portrait. You aren't likely to be a saint, but your heroine is better than you in some significant way, while possessing a weakness you don't. Say she's more adventurous than you, but she's also given to impulsiveness. Or she's more intuitive without being as educated as you are. She's younger and prettier than you, but she's also promiscuous, which you never have been.

You aren't likely to be a sociopath either, but your villain probably is. Imagine a narcissistic, cruel, anti-social, conscienceless, ruthless, violent piece of crap (Mr. or Mrs. Hyde). Surprisingly, it isn't that hard. Just imagine the annoying characteristics you find in yourself and other people, then ratchet them up to a criminal level.

Neither are you a stud, but he isn't hard to imagine. What have you always fantasized a lover would be? Make him better -- but be sure to add some characteristics that annoy you but can be softened, changed, or endured.

And here's where subplots develop organically. All the minor characters revolve around the heroine. They love her or they hate her. They want to kill her or marry her. They gossip about her, or they never seem to notice her. They envy or scorn her. They've been in her life forever or just met her. What each one tries to do for or against her becomes a subplot.

Two minor characters become important in many mysteries: the heroine's friend and the villain's sidekick. The heroine needs someone to confide in; those confidences move the story along, illuminate the heroine's essential character, and convey the author's moral viewpoint. And the sidekick provides a foil for the villain. He might be bad but not as bad as the villain, a sort of watered-down *doppelgänger* or double.

Naming your characters is important. It tells your reader what to think about the character. Roxie Slater sounds lower class; Alexandra Royce sounds upper class. Of course a distinguished name like Dexter Oswald Durbin is funny when attached to an uneducated, heavily tattooed, unprincipled scoundrel. Verlin Dootz Grubbs sounds country. Sterling Steven Wright suggests what he is: Mr. Right. Jerry Lee Grubbs Beaudry sounds like a woman who made her way in life by marrying up. Phil Coker sounds like the cokehead he is. And so on.

Finding your inner Mrs. Hyde, the dark side of self, isn't just a good tip for creating characters. It's good for every aspect of your book.

Tip 8

Select a classic plot

★There aren't a lot to choose from.

The plot is a series of events leading to a resolution. The twists and turns that move the story along keep the reader turning the page. The plot flows from your one-sentence story seed, theme, and lead character. The twists and turns in the plot are important in popular fiction, for genre readers will not tolerate the kind of boredom that "literary" fiction readers will.

The best news for a writer is that there is literally nothing new under the sun, and that goes for plots as well. The number of basic plots is actually very small. Some scholars, like Samuel Johnson, say there are very few without saying how many; other scholars try to put a number on them, generally less than a dozen.

The sources of good plots are readily available to every writer: the Bible, myths, folk and fairy tales, literary classics, plays and musicals, even films. If you want ideas, read widely and watch good movies.

To our minds, the basic plot for a mystery is simple:

★★★Overcoming the monster. Your heroine is in danger, threatened by a monster she must overcome. When she does, she gains something valuable -- perhaps a man's love, great wealth or power, a new family, inner peace, a reputation for wisdom, spiritual redemption, or self-knowledge.

The monster is a **person** -- say, a husband, boyfriend, financial advisor, mother, neighbor, boss, or friend. The mystery about the monster is anything you want it to be: who he is, what makes him tick, how he conceals his true character, what he'll do next, whether the heroine will identify him before he kills her. Even if the monster is existential or abstract -- say, the sudden loss of social standing -- it has to be embodied in a person to be interesting.

The **threat** from the monster is anything you want it to be, but it has to be elemental and gripping: bodily harm or death, financial ruin, defamation, and moral corruption come to mind.

The heroine may **overcome** the monster through her own efforts, as is common in the novels of Mary Higgins Clark and Jane Stanton Hitchcock, or with the help of someone else, perhaps a detective or a boyfriend or even a mysterious stranger.

The **valuable** thing the heroine gains by overcoming the monster needs to be something more than the restoration of the normal order. Perhaps she has a new understanding of human nature, or inherits a fortune, or recognizes the man she should have married -- or something else that matters to you.

If you choose **Overcoming the Monster** as your main plot, the other basic plots are useful as subplots in a mystery novel.

***Beauty and the beast.** An innocent person transforms a monster through love. Example: Charlotte Bronte's *Jane Eyre*.

***Help from a stranger.** A stranger appears out of nowhere, assists in overcoming the danger or in solving a mystery, and then vanishes. Example: *Shane*, the story of the Good Samaritan.

***Quest for a prize.** An adventurer leaves his comfort zone and travels a long distance to achieve an important goal or prize. The destination may be exotic, abnormal, or even magical, and the adventurer may or may not return. Examples: *Raiders of the Lost Ark*, Daniel Defoe's *Robinson Crusoe*, the story of Abram/

Abraham in Genesis.

Redemption or Apocalypse. A person is saved from a nightmare or evil spell, madness, or other psychological influence. The redemption may be accomplished through supernatural means or human intervention, as in Charles Dickens' *A Christmas Carol,* the story of Job, the flight of Joseph and Mary into Egypt, and *Sleeping Beauty.* Or the lifting of the spell may lead to apocalypse, the final destruction, as in Kurt Vonnegut's *Cat's Cradle.*

Rags to riches. An ordinary person gains wealth in an unexpected way. Example: *Cinderella*, the story of Jacob in Genesis.

Ugly duckling. A loser or scapegoat or nobody is transformed into a winner. Example: the story of David and Goliath.

Revenge. A person who has been wronged gets revenge in an unexpected way. Example: Jane Stanton Hitchcock's *Social Crimes* and *One Dangerous Lady.*

This list of plots is suggestive, not prescriptive. But you'll find it easier to construct a coherent plot if you keep its main elements in mind.

Tip 9

Stick with the classic plot structure

★Beginning, middle, and end.

Many learned essays and hundreds of book are written about the intricacies of structuring a plot. Terms like arc, climax, inciting incident, stasis, trigger, comic relief, subplot, dénouement, deus ex machina, prologue, and epilogue make plots seem difficult to construct, something only an academic could do.

In fact, the classic plot structure is very simple. It has three parts: a beginning, a middle, and an end. The three-part structure is classic because it's organic and works both for the author and the reader. Sometimes this structure is called the narrative arc, a pattern of rising and falling action.

There are no rules for how long each of the three parts should be. Their length depends on the story you have to tell and how you tell it, but we find it helpful to think of each as roughly a third of the book, while other writers think of the middle as two-thirds of the story.

But before we discuss the beginning, middle, and end, we need to decide what the mystery is. If the story is about a woman facing a monster, will the reader know who the monster is before the final scenes or not? If the reader knows who the monster is early on, then what's the mystery? In our first novel, *Face Off,* the astute reader can guess the identity of the monster from the first chapter, but the reader doesn't know whether the heroine will fall in love with him or survive the experience if she does, whether she will figure out who he is in time to save herself, or how the monster will try to kill her. We constructed the plot that way deliberately because we wanted the identity of the monster to be plausible, which isn't always the case. Getting into the mind of a monster is interesting.

But in our third novel, *Murder for Old Times' Sake,* we conceal the murderer's identity until the last few chapters. While this is a classic murder plot in the tradition of Agatha Christie, we found it a challenge to explain the monster's nature in a satisfying way without revealing his identity too soon. We tried to do that in a number of ways that may help you: we gave the monster other prominent failings to distract from the greater sin of being a murderer (think Dr. Jekyll); he wasn't the only male character to know the victims or engage in jogging; and we delved into his thoughts (using third-person perspective) in a chapter describing his peculiar hobbies and the murder he's just committed without disclosing identifying details.

***The Beginning: Normal Life Interrupted

The beginning of a novel is normal life interrupted by design or chance. Some writers like Nigel Watts think of normal, everyday life as stasis and the event that changes everything as the trigger. Other writers refer to the beginning as exposition -- a narrative establishing the characters, the setting, and the mood.

Our first book opens with a portrait of the woman and her life and two other lead characters. On the whole the heroine's life is good. She's young, pretty, healthy, and intelligent. She has a good job. She has inherited a little money and a comfortable house in Indiana. She's in love with her college boyfriend, and now that he's gotten a good gig in a rock band, expects him to propose. Twice a year, she vacations with her sister in Florida.

But her life isn't perfect. She's about to get a boss who's difficult to work for. Instead of giving her an engagement ring, her boyfriend dumps her. She's lonely and is ready to get married. She's tired of Indiana weather. Her sister, who is also her best friend, lives so far away she only sees her twice a year.

The other central characters are the two eligible men she's about to meet. One is a very rich and charming surgeon whose wife has just drowned. He has a good life, but it isn't complete without a beautiful young wife. The other is a detective fresh from a broken engagement and still struggling to build his investigative agency. He likes his career but is ready to get married to a more conventional woman than his ex-fiancée.

The event that changes the heroine's life is a Christmas vacation in Florida with her sister. There, she glimpses a new and better life and impulsively decides to move to a better climate, change jobs, forget her old boyfriend, and see what comes of her new relationships.

To sum up, Part One -- the beginning of the novel -- describes the heroine's normal life and the event or circumstance that changes everything. It sets the scene for what must change in the lives of other characters too. In doing so, the monster is introduced without the heroine's necessarily recognizing him as a monster.

***The Middle: New Life Complicated

The middle of the novel is what happens next once normal life has been interrupted. The new, changed life is complicated. Think of the middle of the book as a web of conflicts and obstacles, one twist or surprise following another.

In our first novel, our heroine's life changes because of loss: the death of her parents, the breakup with her boyfriend, and her impending loss of a comfortable career. Her losses are mirrored by those suffered by other important characters she meets: the death of the surgeon's wife, and the detective's decision to break off his engagement.

While on vacation at her sister's house, our heroine impulsively decides to give up her job, cut off all communication with her ex-boyfriend, and move to Florida. She has met the surgeon and the detective in very different circumstances. Both are romantically interested in her, but for different reasons, and her boyfriend continues to pursue her, though not with marriage on his mind. Our heroine thinks she knows the surgeon and the detective pretty well, and she's interested in both. That ends Part One.

In Part Two -- the middle of the story -- our heroine realizes she doesn't know either man the way she thought she did. The men's true characters are gradually revealed to the reader, though not to her. When our heroine eventually chooses one of the three men to marry, her decision is based on false information and reveals how fixated she is on getting married before she's thirty. How the new husband kept his past a secret for so long and how it's uncovered form a subplot. The Hollywood client of the detective forms another subplot that intertwines like a serpent with the lives of not just the heroine but many other characters as well.

Some writers (again like Nigel Watts) think of the stages of the middle of a novel as the quest, a series of both good and bad surprises, and a critical choice to take one path or another. Though we didn't know about Nigel Watts when we wrote *Face Off*, that's not a bad way to describe our novel. Our heroine embarks on quest for a husband, is surprised to discover what she thinks she knows about the characters of the three men in her life, and based on that erroneous knowledge finally chooses one of them to marry.

Many self-help manuals suggest the middle of the novel is the hardest part of the story to write because it can become boring, especially if it's the longest part. We haven't found that to be true. The middle of the story is where the conflicts among characters get ratcheted up and surprises occur. That's why you don't want to write your story exactly as you experienced it. Make it more frightening or more exciting. Multiply the desperate situations, the evil opponents. Include lots of conflict.

To sum up (again using the monster plot), the middle of the novel describes the heroine's torturous path in trying to identify the monster before falling into his clutches.

***The End: The New Normal

The end is the climax, the resolution of all the conflicts: How does the villain go about accomplishing his dastardly intentions? How does the heroine see what is happening and try to protect herself? Will she live or die? If she lives, what will her new life be like? Will the villain be exposed and punished? Nigel Watts calls these stages the climax, reversal, and resolution.

The climax of the novel needs to be unexpected but plausible. In ancient Greek drama, especially the plays of Euripides, the conflict would be resolved in an unexpected and often incredible way, perhaps a crane lowering to the stage a whole new character with no plausible motive for being present. Modern readers don't like that, but they like surprises. To our minds, in the best endings the heroine is saved and the villain punished by something the villain did with entirely different intentions. In our first book, *Face Off*, the heroine is saved by something the villain provided accidentally and he dies as a consequence of events he himself set in motion.

To sum up, Part Three -- the end of the novel -- shows the final resolution, the climax, of the events that were set into motion when the heroine embarked on a different course in life. By overcoming the monster, our heroine has achieved a reversal of fortune or a new normal -- a very different life from anything she could have foreseen.

Tip 10

Hook the reader any way you can

*And there are lots of ways.

In addition to the classic plot structure, we like a prologue to hook the reader and an epilogue to satisfy her curiosity -- and hook her to read our next book. We also like chapter titles because on a Kindle the reader can click on the title and go to the chapter she wants to reread. Introductory quotations are unnecessary but we like them as another dimension for thinking about the story. And recurring characters -- if they're interesting enough -- can create a loyal fan-base.

***Prologue

A prologue is simply a short introduction or preface. It can be an event that precedes the events of the novel, but it doesn't have to be. Its purpose is to hook the reader into reading your book.

For a mystery novel, a good prologue is a short scene that establishes a mystery the reader wants to read about, a puzzle she wants to solve.

Here are some examples: A strange boat crashing into their boat lift interrupts a couple's peaceful evening on their lanai. A retired policeman walking with his dog on the beach finds the remains of a body torn apart by bears. In an old farm pond, a construction crew finds a rusted car, with a body in the trunk. A hotel maid finds a guest dead in the shower she was about to clean. Suddenly a body falls from a high-rise onto a busy sidewalk. A stranger in a hotel lobby, holding a briefcase with a gun concealed inside, furtively watches a beautiful woman check in. Upon arrival in Detroit, a stowaway is found dead in the the hold of an airplane.

In our first novel, the prologue describes the surgeon's boat as it crashes into a boat life. There's a man's head in the water and a woman floating in the channel. Neither is identified. The man, obviously, is dead, but who is he and what led to the crash? The woman might or might not be alive. Who is she and can she be rescued?

None of these suggested prologues literally occurs before the novel starts. Instead, they are taken from the middle or end of the novel. They're integral to the action but ambiguous enough that the reader cannot guess who the person is, how his death occurred, or what it means. They're so exciting (we hope) that the reader can't wait to read the rest of the book.

The prologue is the hook.

***The Epilogue

An epilogue is simply a short description of what happens later. Its purpose is to satisfy the reader's curiosity about the lives of the characters who have survived and hook the reader into reading your next book, especially if it will feature the same characters.

Have you ever watched a true-crime show where after the murderer is apprehended, tried, and sentenced, the fates of all the other people are described in a line or two? The murderer's mother commits suicide. His wife files for divorce. His children are adopted by a relative and change their names. The friend who turned him in moves to another state. The detective is promoted. The local reporter writes a best-seller about the murder.

That's an epilogue: the tying up of loose threads and the creation of a new hook for the next novel. An epilogue isn't necessary, but it's fun to write and fun to read.

In our first novel, the heroine rents a house, sells off all her dead husband's possessions, and tries to decide whether to live the easy life of a wealthy woman or start a new career. The suitor she rejected comes back into her life but it's too early to become romantic with him. A friend who once wrote an anonymous gossip column has the chance to write a best-seller based on the crimes of the dead husband.

The hook to the next novel is obvious. What will the heroine do about her career? Will she marry the once-rejected suitor? Will the reporter become famous?

You don't have to write that next book, but you can if you want to, and if your first book was exciting enough, you have a guaranteed readership for the next one.

We include epilogues simply because we like to read them and are writing for readers like us. Once the mystery has been solved, what in fact happens to the main characters? Novels with literary pretensions often leave the reader hanging on the theory that ambiguity is "deep." Readers of mysteries like ambiguity in the middle of the book but not at the end.

***Chapter Titles.** Many authors don't provide chapter titles, and there's nothing wrong with that. But we like them both as writers and readers. A good chapter title amuses the reader or enlightens her or provokes her interest.

As writers, we like titles because they focus us on the point of the chapter, reminding us of what has to happen to move the plot along and illuminate the principal characters. That doesn't mean we write the chapter title before writing the chapter itself. If no title suggests itself after we've written the chapter, we know it's unfocused and needs some serious rewriting.

***Introductory Quotations.** Introductory quotations aren't necessary either, but we've always liked them for the same reason we like chapter titles. With the availability of Google, apt quotations are easy to find. In our second book, *Monuments to*

Murder, we use two quotations to introduce each of the three parts. For Part One, we selected a quote from George Bernard Shaw approving the elimination of people who are more trouble than they're worth (in his opinion, of course) and an excerpt from the book of James in the Bible warning of the evils of envy and selfish ambition. One quote is ironic, reflecting the view of the murderer; the other embodies our point of view.

***Recurring Characters. If you're writing a traditional detective novel, and if readers like your detective, by all means have him appear in your next book. Lucas Davenport is a winner for John Sandford. Stuart Woods' popular character Stone Barrington has many loyal fans.

Even if you don't have a traditional detective, any appealing character or setting might inspire the next book and a loyal readership. Sometimes one of your minor characters will strike a chord you didn't expect. Dex Durbin in our first novel is so disturbingly appealing that a number of our readers have told us they hope to see him again.

Tip 11

Choose a setting you know

*But throw in some spice.

Settings are important to provide ambiance and underscore the essential elements of character and plot. Like everything else, the setting suggests itself once you have the story seed.

If you've never been to Bratislava, don't set your main story there. It's too hard to make the story vivid and realistic, and if you've never been there, the setting probably adds nothing to the story anyway Choose a setting you know for the main events.

That doesn't mean your characters can't travel to places you've never been. Readers like an exotic or historical or glamorous or frightening setting as a change of pace. And you can find out all you need to know for a chapter or two about the Red Rock country around Sedona, Arizona or the streets of Paris or a remote castle in Scotland by watching travel films, reading travel literature, and talking to friends who've been there. Google and Wikipedia are great helps.

We set our first two books in southwest Florida because we like to visit Marco Island and Naples and imagine ourselves living on the seashore in sunshine among palm trees. Our characters take jaunts to Savannah for a movie premiere, Hollywood for an actor's memorial, the mountains of Tennessee for the outing of a secret, and Paris for a honeymoon because those settings were natural to the characters and enhanced the plot. Besides, we know those places and like them.

We set our third novel in Fort Wayne, Indiana because that's where we live and mystery novels are never set in flyover country, though given the vast number of mystery fans in the Midwest, they should be. Again our characters spend some time at a spa in Sedona; in a literary agent's office, a luxurious hotel, and a famous museum in New York City; and a creepy lodge in the Upper Peninsula of Michigan. Because we like to move around in real life, we assume our readers like to move around in our novels.

Tip 12

Find your voice

*Speak naturally.

Much is written about whether to write in the first person or third person, whether to write from an omniscient point of view or not, whether to speak directly to the reader or only through characters. Make it easy for yourself. Think of the books you've most enjoyed reading.

First-person point of view simply means one character tells the story as if writing in a diary. That voice can come from the main character or from a narrator-as-observer. "I did this, I said that, I heard a strange noise." Most books are not written in the first person, and many readers dislike it. But first person is appropriate where the emphasis is on the interior life and peculiar perspective of one character. *The Lovely Bones* by Alice Sebold is a good example. In *The Great Gatsby,* the narrator's perspective adds moral nuance to an otherwise hackneyed story. (Many critics will have apoplexy at the charge of "hackneyed" in reference to F. Scott Fitzgerald.)

Third person means the author is God. "Sally wandered into the street." "Harry scratched his head." "Barry was nervous." It allows you as the author to convey some of the interior life, the unspoken thoughts, the secret actions, the suppressed feelings of characters whose full story cannot be told through their spoken words and actions. Using the third person also means that no one character has to see everything, hear everything, know everything -- a valuable perspective in a murder mystery.

Second-person point of view is rare in fiction. "You are standing on the bridge." "You aren't this kind of woman." It could be a fine change of pace, but normally second person is used in things like manuals (such as this tip sheet) instructing you what to do. If you want to test the effect of the second-person point of view in a novel, check out *Bright Lights, Big City* by Jay McInerney.

If one character is special, scenes featuring that character can be written in first-person while writing others in third. We did that at the end of our second novel, and Kathryn Stockett does it in *The Help*.

For us, third person is the most natural voice and the most useful for writing a mystery novel. As readers, we like to get into the heads and hearts of all the characters. And omniscience is handy, so a scene involving more than one character -- which is almost all scenes -- can convey the inner thoughts of everyone, as needed.

Tip 13

Tell the story chronologically

★But tell it from many perspectives.

The mystery story can be told in any sequence you want, but it's annoying to read a book where you have no idea where you are in time or place. Story-telling gymnastics and experiments with time are tolerated -- even venerated -- in "literary" novels, like those of William Faulkner and James Joyce, but not in most genre fiction, except for sci-fi novels. The point of writing a commercial mystery novel is to get it bought and read by lots of readers, not studied for its shocking originality by a couple of high-brows in academic circles. (We say this with all due respect to literary idols and high-brow academics, of course.)

So -- except for the prologue (see **Tip 10**) -- tell the story as the events naturally unfold. That doesn't mean you can't weave in the back stories of your characters as the back story is relevant. In fact, setting out the biography of each character in a narrative is boring. Work in the details as they make sense.

We find it boring to stay with one character, however, and we don't like long chapters. So in our first novel our heroine gets on a plane to go to Florida on a Sunday morning just before Christmas. Her life is going to change there, and many other people are going to enter her life. In the boarding area of the airport, she meets a stranger who later plays a big role in her life. Meanwhile, in

Florida, on that same Sunday, a low-life couple, both of whom are connected to the man who will become her husband, argue in a hot tub. Then two women -- one of whom will eventually be a witness to the boat accident that almost takes our heroine's life (as the prologue has shown) and the younger woman we met in the hot tub -- run into each other in a bikini shop. That chance meeting reveals not only something about the younger woman but about the man who will become the heroine's husband.

In real life, we're focused on our own life as if it were the only one being lived. We know other people are living their lives too, but we don't know what they're doing at any given moment, what they're saying about us, how they're plotting against us (if they are), or how their lives are affecting us. In a novel, we can find out.

So we write short chapters, switching from one person's perspective to another. Each chapter ends with a hook: an action yet to be taken, a confrontation yet to occur, a promise yet to be fulfilled, another shoe about to be dropped. That way the reader can't put the book down (or so some of them tell us).

Tip 14

Focus on dialogue and action

*But use narrative when it works.

You can tell the story through narrative, dialogue, and action.

***Narrative, or exposition, is simply an account, a story, the representation of action without dialogue. It's useful and necessary to any story, especially for skipping the boring bits, such as the irrelevant trivialities of an important conversation between characters. Narrative is a way to bring in memories and dreams, to recall significant bits of a character's background, or to introduce interesting digressions on bread-making, palm-reading, or antique-shopping. If a character is silently driving somewhere in a hurry, then say so. That's narrative. But if it's possible to interlard some action, such as the driver's frantic attempts to pull up a map on his GPS system, then add that. If he swears to himself or calls his wife, then add some dialogue. In other words, use narrative for economy but break it up with action and dialogue where possible.

This is not to belittle the pleasure of reading narrative or exposition, especially when used to get on with the plot and spare the reader unnecessary details.

***Dialogue is conversation. It's fun to write and fun to read, especially if it involves those conversations we wish we could overhear in real life but almost never do: an eager but shy lover's proposal of marriage, a wife's angry tirade when she learns of her husband's infidelity, a girlfriend's disbelief upon hearing her boyfriend has a dead body in his truck, a mother's confession to her son that she killed his father, a double agent's disclosure of false information.

Credible, authentic dialogue is hard to write but it gets easier with practice. Listen to your characters as if you were really talking to them. Say the words aloud as you write them. Use contractions where people normally use them -- don't, can't, I'd, should've, what'd. Use elisions (the omission of words and sounds) where people normally use them when speaking -- "Makes no sense" instead of "That doesn't make sense." Even very literate people make grammatical errors, use the wrong word, and utter incomplete or run-on sentences when they talk, so write dialogue that way so it doesn't sound stilted. Elmore Leonard is famous for his dialogue.

When many years ago the Scribe first tried her hand at writing (very bad) fiction, she thought each character should sound completely different from all the other characters, but that's not true, or even comfortable to read. Nevertheless, one person's conversation shouldn't sound exactly like another's. Characters have different backgrounds, interests, and education. To emphasize a special trait, you might give a character a catch-phrase or tag: One of our criminals always says, "I know that for a fact." Another says, "Know that." One doctor calls men "old chap"; another calls them "my friend." An uneducated man misuses words -- axtortion for extortion, revelant for relevant -- and he has a habit of pointing his index finger at people as if it were a gun. If not overdone, the catch-phrases, misused words, and habitual actions identify the speaker, reveal something about him, and amuse the reader.

Dialects are colorful but hard to write. Kathryn Stockett does it well in *The Help* and Elmore Leonard does it well in every book he writes. Unless you have a very good ear, don't try, but if you know the dialect well, go for it.

Introducing dialogue, identifying the speaker, and describing his mood can get repetitive and awkward, so rather than use the first example over and over, try the second once in awhile:

   1 - Louie said, "Pass me the salt." He looked murderously angry.
   2 - Louie eyed the salt. "Pass me that or I'll kill you."
   3- "Pass me the salt," Louie said murderously.

There's nothing wrong with the first sentence at all. It's just that he said, she said, he said gets old -- though, of course, you can't leave the reader confused about who said what. The emotion that goes with the spoken words is best conveyed in the words themselves, or in the context and action of the character. The third phrase is just awful. The better you describe the context and the more revealing the dialogue is, the fewer adverbs you'll have to use to convey emotion.

Sometimes a person talks to himself without saying anything out loud. Knowing that helps the reader. We simply put a character's thoughts in italics to differentiate them from spoken words.

Budding writers sometimes tell us they've written whole scenes of characters talking, then realized the passages were pointless and tossed them out. It's tempting, but you'll avoid the pitfall if you remember that dialogue has a function. It tells the story by creating conflict, revealing earlier events, creating sympathy (or antipathy) for a character, or moving the plot forward. It reveals a character's emotions, motives and mood. It reminds the reader of something she might have forgotten or foreshadows future events. It pulls the reader into the heart of the story and the author's moral universe.

If the dialogue doesn't perform one of those functions, cross it out. And if when you read it aloud it sounds awkward, rewrite.

***Action** makes the story exciting, pulling the reader in. It breaks up chunks of dialogue or narrative. Rather than tell the reader that Roxie is a self-absorbed, uneducated slut, show her in a tiny bikini pirouetting in front of a mirror, shaking her long hair around, mispronouncing the name of Pucci, and making suggestive remarks about the surgeon who gave her the new boobs she's displaying. Rather than telling the reader how brave Tom is, let *him* tell the story of foiling a murderous husband's plot to kill his wife as a way of explaining the bullet hole in his overnight bag -- or, if it's appropriate, show the scene as it unfolded.

In other words, show the story rather than just telling it. One way to do that is to picture the story in your head as if it were a film. What are the characters doing? Is it day or night? Hot or cold? Are they eating or pacing or partying? How are they feeling? What's the setting look, smell, and sound like?

A helpful way to portray action is to write short, vivid scenes. We picture all the action that way, again (not to belabor the point) as if we were shooting a movie. Say a doctor decides to kill the detective he's hired. The scene takes place on a cigarette boat in the Gulf of Mexico on a night without moonlight. What are the characters wearing? What's the temperature? How fast is the boat going and what does it sound like? What warning song plays through the detective's head? What ruse does the doctor use to make the detective vulnerable? What does the detective experience as he's thrown off his feet? What does the doctor say to cover his murderous intentions?

Tip 15

Don't skip the humor

*Life is funny.

Mysteries are serious business. Bad things happen. People die, lose their reputations and fortunes, or sink into moral decay. Now that's funny.

Seriously, a dark story told darkly from beginning to end is truly deadly -- unless, of course, it's "literature."

Some critics think tragedy is tragedy and comedy is comedy, and every written work must be consistent in tone from one end to the other. But Shakespeare didn't, and if he can get a laugh from Sir John Falstaff in the *Henry IV* plays, which are definitely not comedies, we mystery authors can try.

Fortunately, murder mysteries are neither strictly tragedy nor comedy. True, they're stories of things going wrong -- sometimes deadly wrong. But they're also stories of life in all its craziness, and life is really, really funny. So don't be afraid of humor where it naturally fits the character or circumstance. No need to force it. Let it happen.

When you really think about it, the conventional murder mystery is more comedy than tragedy anyway. The resolution of a conventional murder mystery rewards the protagonist and punishes the villain. That's comedy. By contrast, the resolution of a tragedy ends with the protagonist losing his social standing, his fortune, even his life. In the conventional mystery, those bad things happen only to the villain, and though that's tragedy, it's offset by the good things that happen to the protagonist. On the whole, then, a conventional mystery is more comedy than tragedy.

We love the sharp, zingy one-liners of Ann Coulter and Dave Barry, but writing their kind of humor is not our talent and probably wouldn't work in most mystery novels. Our humor is slyer: pretensions, misused words, unconscious slips of the tongue, a foolish gesture, undeserved self-importance, contradictions between demeanor and intention, misunderstandings, satire, a ridiculous person. Some popular mystery writers would benefit mightily -- in our humble opinion -- from a good dose of humor. Perhaps they should try reading a Jane Austen novel all the way through.

Tip 16

Catch a rising star

*With a captivating title.

We all know titles are important. Should you choose a title before your write the book, or after, or whenever it occurs to you? What should it signal? How do you choose it? How you can be sure it's unique?

We suggest starting everything with the story seed, the one-sentence summary of your book. The title follows from that: a character, a catch-phrase, a setting, an action.

For our second book, the Story-Teller already had in mind the tale of an ambitious, over-bearing stage mother when we visited Bonaventure Cemetery in Savannah. It is breathtakingly beautiful and a just a little creepy, replete with gorgeous monuments and bountiful nature but also replete, of course, with the dead. The idea for the title of *Monuments to Murder* arose there. The ambitious stage mother would be famous for her magnificent gardens, where the monuments scattered throughout the grounds secretly signaled the murderous extent of her ambition. The title -- and the book cover featuring a beautiful angel statue against a lush cemetery background-- naturally followed.

Then we checked Amazon to see if our working title had already been taken. It hadn't. We recommend that step to avoid confusion with other authors. For our third book, we considered a title like *A Murder of Crows* but found several other books with that title -- of course. The phrase was too good and too obvious not to have been adopted by somebody.

Most mystery fiction titles are short, suggest mystery or even murder, and catch the imagination. If the title is not invented out of whole cloth, it can be taken from a fairy tale, a nursery rhyme, a well-known poem, a familiar saying, a popular song, a Shakespearean play, or a Bible story. If you plan a series featuring a special character, consider doing what Janet Evanovich does. She uses a sequence of numbered titles, starting with one and progressing to the current eighteen, for her Stephanie Plum series. The alphabet sequence comes to mind too, or the main ingredient in a featured recipe, or the caliber of a gun, or an historical artifact, or the name of a key setting or character.

The title you use may or may not signal that the book is a murder mystery. If it doesn't, then you can always add a tag line like "A Mystery Novel" or "A Novel of Murder." In any case, once you publish, your novel will be appropriately categorized as belonging to a particular genre.

Our recommendation is to take the title from the story seed, make it short, suggest mystery, and check to be sure it's unique. We have no advice on when to choose the title. We've done it at the beginning, at the end, and in the middle.

Tip 17

Keep the prose real and edit viciously

*Purple is *not* the new black.

Many words have been written about the importance of the first and last sentences in a novel. They are important, but you'll probably end up revising them anyway, so don't sweat them. Just start writing.

And don't worry about writing sentences so memorable they're quoted everywhere. That isn't what mystery readers are looking for. They're looking for an absorbing story told in good, understandable English.

Caveat: If you haven't mastered grammar, syntax, word usage, and punctuation, then bone up on them or find an editor. If your vocabulary comprises a few thousand words, mostly of the profane or one-syllable variety, writing a book really isn't your thing anyway.

We're assuming you're literate and are well-acquainted with the basics of good writing. Then keep the prose real. Don't write long, florid descriptions of people's looks or the setting. A few well-chosen words are all you need to describe a busy Paris street or a scary biker bar. If a character looks like a famous person, say so. Describing a sex scene in graphic detail or with flowery euphemisms may titillate bodice-ripper fans but disgust the mystery reader. (Stuart Woods would disagree, of course, at least as to the graphic part.)

Metaphors (and similes, which are a type of metaphor), plus other figures of speech, leaven the prose and give insight into character, but don't search overlong for them or make up silly ones. Examples:

Pretty good: He studied her as if she were a reptile long thought to be extinct. [She's unattractive and scary.]
The wrestler's head was squared off like a block of stone. [He's big and scary and might not be the sharpest tool in the drawer.]
Suddenly, she saw the light. [Meaning she saw the truth.]

Pretty bad: He thought of her as the rare old coin he'd bought in an Arab market twenty years earlier and then foolishly lost in a poker game after playing golf all day. [Is she precious or just old and unimportant? Did he lose her because he was forgetful or because he is boring and pompous and treated her like a possession?]

Puns are fun sometimes. A pun is a form of word play suggesting two or more meanings for humorous effect. In our second novel, an actor refers to *cannabis* as *cannablis* to convey the drug's effect and his version of humor -- and not incidentally to irritate the gardener, who insists on proper Latin names. In our first novel, one of the characters is incensed at "axtortion"; his mispronunciation conveys not only his ignorance but also more about his violent character than he knows.

Irony is vital to mysteries and many other genres. Situational irony is a contrast between what we expect to happen and what actually happens. A famous example is Oedipus leaving Corinth for Thebes to avoid fulfilling an oracle that he would kill his father and marry his mother, only to do both in the process. Our first novel, *Face Off*, ends in irony, for the murderer inadvertently provides his intended victim with the means of survival and provokes a gunfight that kills him. What some commentators call a reversal of fortune is in effect an ironic circumstance. Irony can also be verbal. A character faced with having to confer with a hated enemy says, "I'm so thrilled!", meaning the opposite.

Varying the **sentence structure** from subject-verb-object is a must -- remember gerunds and dependent clauses. And contrary to some old-fashioned rules, sentences can begin with a conjunction -- and, but, for, or, etc. Verbs are the most important words you can find, for they make action vivid. Adjectives and adverbs can be used sparingly if your verbs are sharp enough. One sentence should lead smoothly to the next. Run-on sentences often make sense in dialogue, and some writers like Daisy Goodwin in *The American Heiress* get by with them just fine even in narrative.

An author must not only write but **edit**. If you like to write well enough to write a novel, you probably love your own **prose**. That's a mistake. If you're bored reading your own work, if your prose is plodding or awkward, if it isn't lively and interesting, if there are passages you can't bear to reread -- then your reader will be just as bored. When you finish the book (or even a chapter), put on your editor's glasses, pick up a big red marker, grab a cup of strong coffee, pull up your big-girl panties, and start slashing. Be vicious. If you can't edit your own work, find someone who can. The best way to learn to write in a way that carries the reader along is to read good prose, both fiction and non-fiction.

The first complete draft of our first novel was way too long, stuffed with unnecessary back story and irrelevant detail. The Scribe had to delete graceful sentences, beautiful paragraphs, delightful scenes, sometimes whole chapters and even minor characters. She had to rearrange chapters, change characters' names, delete dissertations on this or that, explain motives better, break up narrative, and alter settings.

When she was a young woman, the Scribe would have bristled at the criticism. No more. Writing a novel is not a sacred act, God whispering holy truth into one's ear. It's a flawed human act of imagination that can be improved.

Part Three: Work It

It takes courage to grow up and become who you really are.

e.e. cummings

Tip 18

Eating a whole carcass kills the appetite

*So just start somewhere.

The idea of writing a whole darn book is just overwhelming, you know? So after thinking about the whole darn book, back up and think of it one scene at a time. Write in chunks. Each day your goal is to bite off the next chunk, not to consume the whole carcass. That attitude makes writing more fun than work.

The way the Scribe does it is to sit down at the computer every day at the same time, about nine or ten in the morning and write an entire chapter, sometimes two or three if she's in a good mood, her back doesn't hurt, and somebody doesn't invite her to lunch. Then she makes the revisions the Storyteller in her role as editor delivered earlier. In the afternoon she puts on her editor-spectacles and adds or removes details as necessary from whatever the Storyteller approved.

The Scribe treats writing like a real-life job -- a regular schedule, a set number of hours, a product to be judged by the boss. But it's a fun job. She gets to imagine the playing-out of the Storyteller's brilliant ideas. If you're both the Storyteller and the Scribe, you get double the fun.

A novel needs to be at least 40,000 words. Our third novel is about three times that length, filling 209 single-spaced computer pages using 12-point font, or about 535 words per page. Our chapters average about 1,435 words each, or slightly less than three pages. Writing one chapter a day five days a week means the book can be completed in about fifteen weeks or roughly four months. Assume another month for scheduling mishaps and goofing off and another month for editing. If you keep to that schedule, you aren't looking at a project that's years in the making. It's done in six months, from the first word on the paper to publishing on Kindle.

Think of it. Nine months for a baby, only six months for a book! Any woman can do that while planning a holiday party and running for Congress.

Tip 19

Forget literary gurus

★Remember readers like you.

Writing a mystery isn't likely to garner you a lot of respect in academic circles or a thoughtful review in *The New York Times Review*. That's true even if you are lucky enough to get published in paper by a major publishing house. It's especially true If you publish an e-book or an on-demand paperback. The common view is that if you're self-published, you must not be very good. Even your friends and family will view your first effort with skepticism.

The disrespect for e-books and on-demand paperbacks will diminish with time, but the disrespect for genre fiction, whatever form it takes, probably won't.

Genre fiction -- which includes not just mysteries but romances, westerns, fantasy, and science fiction among others -- doesn't generate much respect from the literati. The Scribe actually wrote a doctoral thesis at a respected university on the mystery novels of Ross Macdonald. His detective stories were as wise, well-written, and absorbing as some "high" literature, but they command very little respect among the literati.

In one of the Scribe's oral examinations, she was asked why detective fiction should be taken seriously since life isn't a mystery that gets solved. Her answer was that all fiction is essentially mystery since the reader doesn't know what happens next or there would be no point in reading the whole book, so if one kind of fiction is to be taken seriously, then mysteries should be too. Furthermore, life is a mystery: who confidently predicts his own end? Probably not the best answer, but she was nervous.

So why are murder mysteries not taken seriously by the highbrows among us? We're not sure, but we have a couple of theories.

Consider first the appeal of a mystery. It's elemental -- danger overcome, secrets exposed, justice dealt to the evil-doer and mercy to the other characters. The prose is typically straightforward, colorful but without elaborate verbal gymnastics. The characters are so real, so familiar, the reader thinks she knows them. The timeline is clear from beginning to end. The story rests on a moral foundation of right and wrong: the good guys win, the bad guys perish.

From the point of view of the literati, especially the pagan literati, these elements mean the fiction is too simple and therefore low-brow. In their minds, real life can't be confined to a plot, people are too complex to be understood, and morals and ethics are ambiguous. That may be true of life, but one of the great values of a book is that it's an escape from real life. Furthermore, it's popular to believe that genuine artists are profoundly crazy, not boringly sane, and they don't write to sell, because writing to sell is crass. Again, that may be true of "real" artists, but being just a little depressed or a little neurotic -- which is most of us -- is probably enough to get a good genre novel written and published. And writing to sell is no more crass than writing to be immortalized as "great."

That's one of our theories. Then consider the function of academics and critics. Since genre fiction can be read and appreciated by almost anyone, it leaves nothing for the learned professors and reviewers to do. Their specialized knowledge, years of training, "sophisticated" moral universes, and arcane vocabularies cannot be deployed to dazzle the public or justify their existence.

But don't despair. Writing in a popular genre helps categorize the book for a recognizable market, in the eyes of either an agent or reader. Furthermore, some mysteries and other genre novels do get reviewed, and some genre writers are accorded respect. Even superb newspapers like *The Wall Street Journal* occasionally take notice of genre fiction and e-books.

Nevertheless, unless you're a genius about to write The Great American Novel (in which case you shouldn't be reading this little tip sheet anyway), don't write for the literati, or even for yourself to indulge a fantasy. Write for your readers.

Tip 20

Keep your eyes on the prize

★And the main prize isn't money -- really.

The prize is actually writing a book and then publishing it for a commercial audience instead of just dreaming about it. Money is a welcome by-product of reaching a lot of readers. Appreciating money is good; loving it isn't.

Of course, you hope to make some money from your writing. But thousands of other authors do too. You're competing with a lot of talented writers for a finite pool of readers, and as we've mentioned, marketing isn't easy for the average e-book author. So expecting to get rich by writing a book isn't realistic -- though it can certainly happen. Of course, there will be no money at all unless you sit down and give it a try. Write, write, write.

Scorning money by pretending it doesn't matter is just as lethal as worshipping it. Your novel will be better if you focus on making it salable -- that is, appealing to a large number of discerning readers. Ignoring the salability of a novel allows you to be sloppy and self-indulgent. You please only yourself. You create unappealing characters, tell boring stories, parade specialized knowledge, write awkward sentences, employ poor grammar, and stud the story with unnecessary, off-putting screeds about your politics or religion or peculiar hobbies.

Rather than writing solely to get rich or pretending money

means nothing at all, focus on the fun of writing for happy, loyal readers. That focus will ensure an entertaining book with the potential to sell a million copies. Even if the book doesn't sell well, at least you'll have something to be proud of.

Tip 21

Shoot the incubus!

*Free yourself from doubt.

If you've never written a book before -- and why else would you be reading this? -- there's probably a very stern critic squatting on your shoulder like an incubus whispering, "You can't do it." The incubus might have the face of a parent, a professor, even a friend. He sat on the Scribe's shoulder for fifty years.

This tip may seem to contradict **Tip 3** about getting over yourself. But it doesn't. Wanting all the praise for yourself, on the one hand, and being afraid even to try a new enterprise, on the other, are simply two extremes of attitude that do a person no good. Be humble enough to find whatever storytelling, writing, or editing help you need, and then get to work.

There are probably many ways to kill the incubus -- psychotherapy, meditation, strong drink, prayer, finding a mentor, signing up for a literary retreat in New Hampshire. But there's only one sure way we personally know about. Just start writing. Stop talking about how someday you'll do it.

Forget the agents and publishers who aren't likely to read anything you submit as a first-time author anyway. Forget the critics who scorn commercial genre fiction. Forget the rules of the professor who spilled gallons of red ink on your essays and short stories. Forget the friends who can't imagine you as a real author.

In fact, treat books like this as suggestions, not rules. Our tips are meant to help you, but if they don't, make your own way. To prove we mean it, we didn't follow our own rules in our second book, *Monuments to Murder*. There is no prologue. The lead character is an anti-heroine. The epilogue leaves some loose ends -- well, loose. At least in our minds, the flouting of some of our "rules" was necessary to tell the story the way it needed to be told.

So free yourself.

Shoot the incubus.

Then find Mrs. Hyde -- your inner evil doppelgänger -- and let her loose!

Glossary of Literary Terms

Antagonist: The protagonist's arch enemy, the villain, often the source of conflict.

Arc: A pattern of rising and falling action (or victory and defeat), either in a character's development or in the unfolding of the plot.

Catharsis: Purging of emotion, typically in Part 3 (the end) of a novel.

Characters: Imaginary figures rendered as real persons, preferably well-rounded in order to drive the plot.

Climax: The most dramatic part of a story, occurring in Part 3 (the end) of a novel, where all the conflicts come to a head.

Dénouement: A French word meaning the untying of knots; the conclusion of the story; often the same as the resolution or catastrophe ending a story and unraveling mysteries; an example is the boating accident that concludes *Face Off* or (not to compare the two works) the final scene of Shakespeare's *As You Like It*.

Deus ex machina: A plot device (literally meaning "god out of the machine"), common in Greek tragedy and sometimes used in modern literature, by which an unexpected event changes the otherwise inevitable outcome of a story, as in *Lord of the Flies* where a passing navy man rescues the children who are so savage they'd otherwise kill each other; in modern literature, the device is expected to be plausible.

Dialogue: Characters' spoken words, but more focused than real conversation; enclosed in double quotation marks if spoken aloud; may be rendered in italics if unspoken thought.

Dramatic structure: A plot divided into parts, usually (but not always) three parts: a beginning, a middle, and an end.

Epilogue: A short summation at the end of a novel explaining what happened to the characters after the climax, tying up any loose ends.

Exposition: Introductory background information provided largely in narrative form, especially in Part 1 (the beginning).

Falling action: Unraveling of conflict, typically in Part 3 (the end).

Genre: A category of popular fiction, such as mystery, fantasy, romance, or science fiction, featuring certain conventions in style, subject, and point of view; differentiated from "literary fiction."

Incubus: A mythological male demon who corrupts the victim, in this case, any authority or judgmental figure who makes you think you can't write a novel.

Irony: Contrast between what is expected to happen and what really happens (situational irony) or between the nominal meaning of words and their underlying meaning (verbal irony).

Literary guru: A person who, if he deigned to read your novel, would know more about it than you do and find much fault.

Metaphor: A figure of speech implicitly comparing one thing to another: "Her eyes were jewels."

Narrative: The narrator's (or author's) expository recounting of events in a story.

Plot: The sequence of events by which the story unfolds, the characters' motives are revealed and their fates determined; the classic plot has three parts, the beginning, middle, and end.

Point of view: The viewpoint from which the story is told: first person (I, we), second person (you), or third person omniscient (he, she, they).

Prologue: A short introduction or preface, setting the mood, posing the puzzle, foreshadowing the plot, or introducing a character, intended to hook the reader.

Prose: A form of written language, common in fiction, using a loose structure and natural flow of words, contrasted with the formal structure and rhythmical flow of poetry.

Protagonist: The lead or central character, either good or bad; sometimes called the hero or anti-hero; mystery fiction typically requires a good protagonist.

Quest: The protagonist's journey to change her life, solve a problem, or find a treasure.

Resolution: See dénouement above; resolution may be comic (favorable to the protagonist), tragic (unfavorable to the protagonist), or neutral (protagonist unchanged); the resolution returns the protagonist to a new, fresh stasis.

Reversal: A change in the status of the characters after the climax in Part 3 (the end) of the story.

Rising action: Increase in conflict, especially in Part 2 (the middle) of a novel.

Setting: The physical or geographic place and the time period in which events occur.

Simile: A figure of speech directly comparing one thing to another using words like "like": "Her eyes sparkled like diamonds."

Stasis: Everyday, normal life, especially in Part 1 (the beginning), characterizing the start of a conventional plot before the lead character encounters a life-changing obstacle or event.

Story seed (not a literary term): A one-sentence statement of the story from which all other elements flow.

Surprise: Unexpected events in Part 2 (the middle) of the story; they can be pleasant or not, but typically in a mystery most involve conflict.

Tags: "He said," "She said," introducing dialogue and identifying the speaker.

Theme: The unifying subject of a novel, especially the moral viewpoint.

Trigger: An event that starts the story in Part 1; often it's beyond the protagonist's control.